NURSERY RHYMES

Illustrated by Eric Kincaid
Compiled by Desmond Marwood

Brown Watson
ENGLAND

CONTENTS

Simple Simon

Simple Simon met a pieman
Going to the fair;
Said Simple Simon to the pieman:
"Let me taste your ware."
Said the pieman to Simple Simon:
"Show me first your penny."
Said Simple Simon to the pieman:
"Indeed, I have not any."

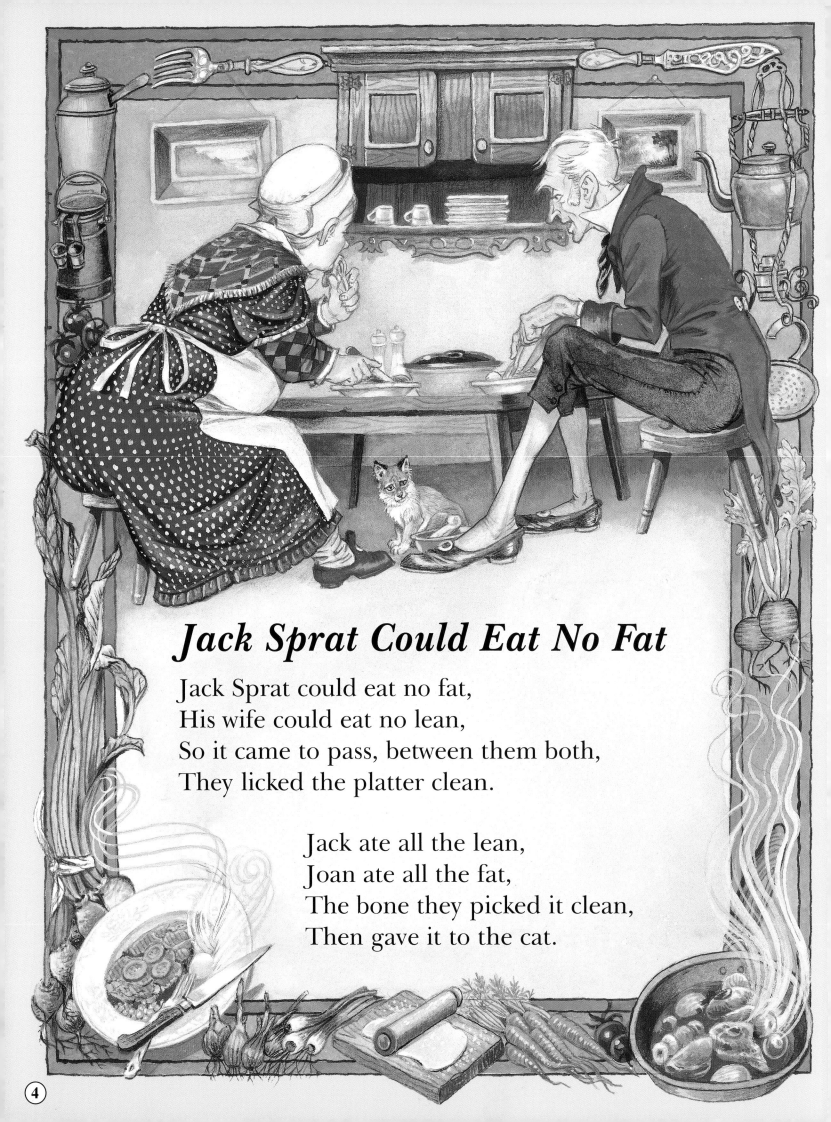

Jack Sprat Could Eat No Fat

Jack Sprat could eat no fat,
His wife could eat no lean,
So it came to pass, between them both,
They licked the platter clean.

Jack ate all the lean,
Joan ate all the fat,
The bone they picked it clean,
Then gave it to the cat.

Hey Diddle, Diddle

Hey diddle, diddle,
The cat and the fiddle,
The cow jumped over the moon.
The little dog laughed
To see such sport,
And the dish ran away with the spoon.

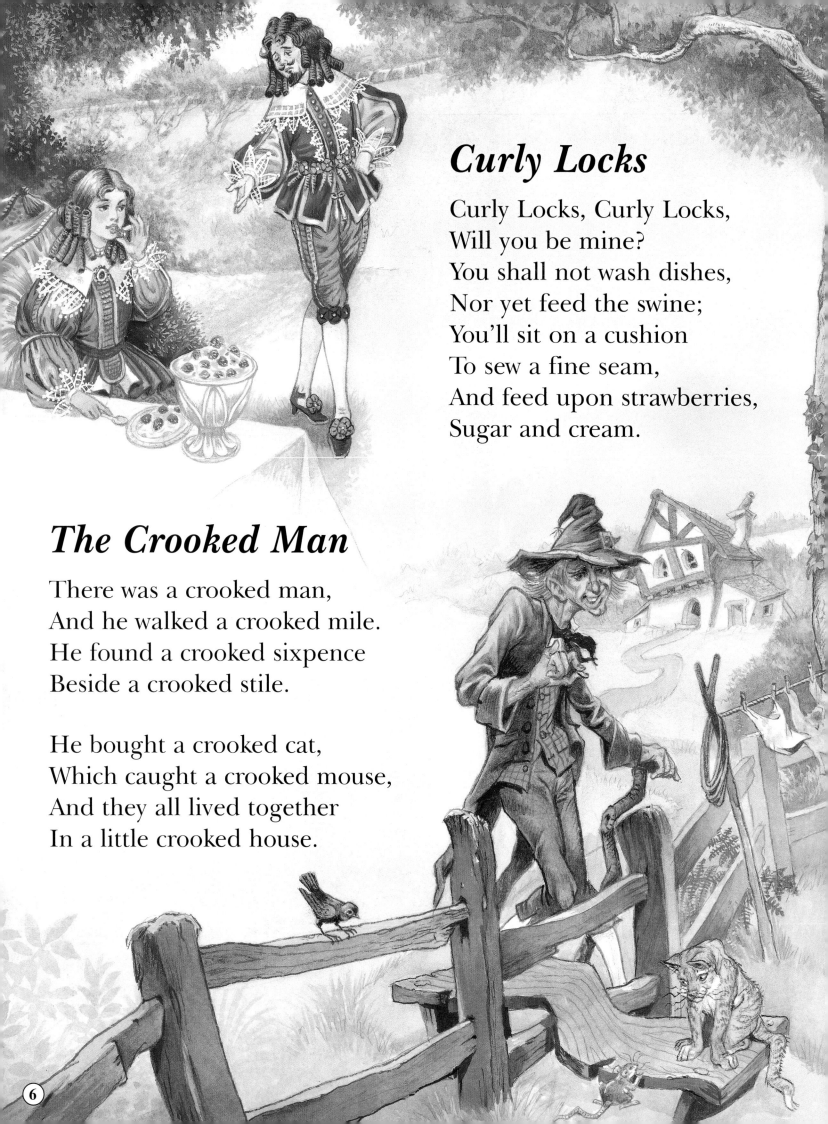

Curly Locks

Curly Locks, Curly Locks,
Will you be mine?
You shall not wash dishes,
Nor yet feed the swine;
You'll sit on a cushion
To sew a fine seam,
And feed upon strawberries,
Sugar and cream.

The Crooked Man

There was a crooked man,
And he walked a crooked mile.
He found a crooked sixpence
Beside a crooked stile.

He bought a crooked cat,
Which caught a crooked mouse,
And they all lived together
In a little crooked house.

Little Bo-Peep

Little Bo-Peep has lost her sheep,
And doesn't know where to find them;
Leave them alone and they'll come home,
Wagging their tails behind them.

There Was an Old Woman

There was an old woman,
Who lived in a shoe,
She had so many children
She didn't know what to do;

She gave them some broth,
Without any bread,
She whipped them all soundly,
And sent them to bed.

8

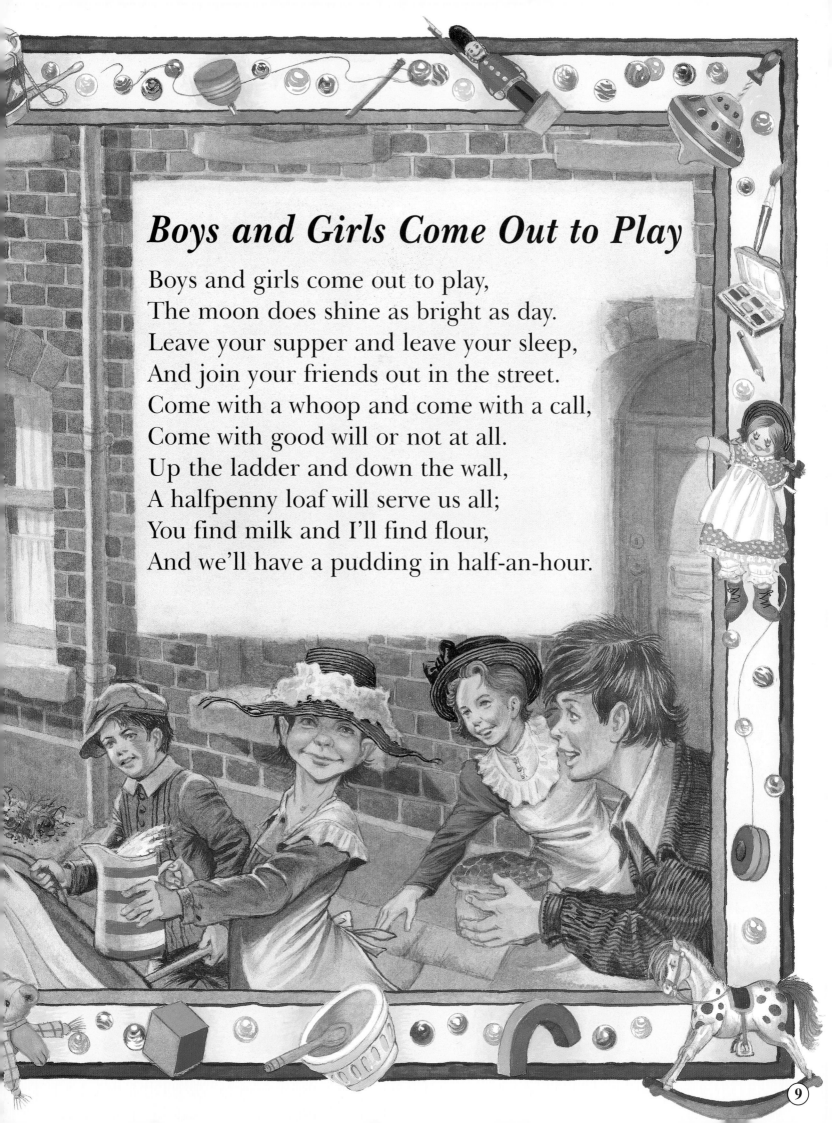

Boys and Girls Come Out to Play

Boys and girls come out to play,
The moon does shine as bright as day.
Leave your supper and leave your sleep,
And join your friends out in the street.
Come with a whoop and come with a call,
Come with good will or not at all.
Up the ladder and down the wall,
A halfpenny loaf will serve us all;
You find milk and I'll find flour,
And we'll have a pudding in half-an-hour.

Ring-a-Ring O'Roses

Ring-a-ring o'roses,
A pocket full of posies,
A-tishoo! A-tishoo!
We all fall down.

Georgie Porgie

Georgie Porgie, pudding and pie,
Kissed the girls and made them cry.
When the boys came out to play,
Georgie Porgie ran away.

Cock-a-Doodle Doo!

Cock-a-doodle doo!
My dame has lost her shoe,
My master's lost his fiddling stick,
And knows not what to do.

Little Tommy Tucker

Little Tommy Tucker sang for his supper,
What shall we give him?
White bread and butter.
How shall he cut it without any knife?
How will he marry, without any wife?

Cobbler, Cobbler

Cobbler, cobbler, mend my shoe,
Get it done by half-past two;
Stitch it up and stitch it down,
Then I'll give you half-a-crown.

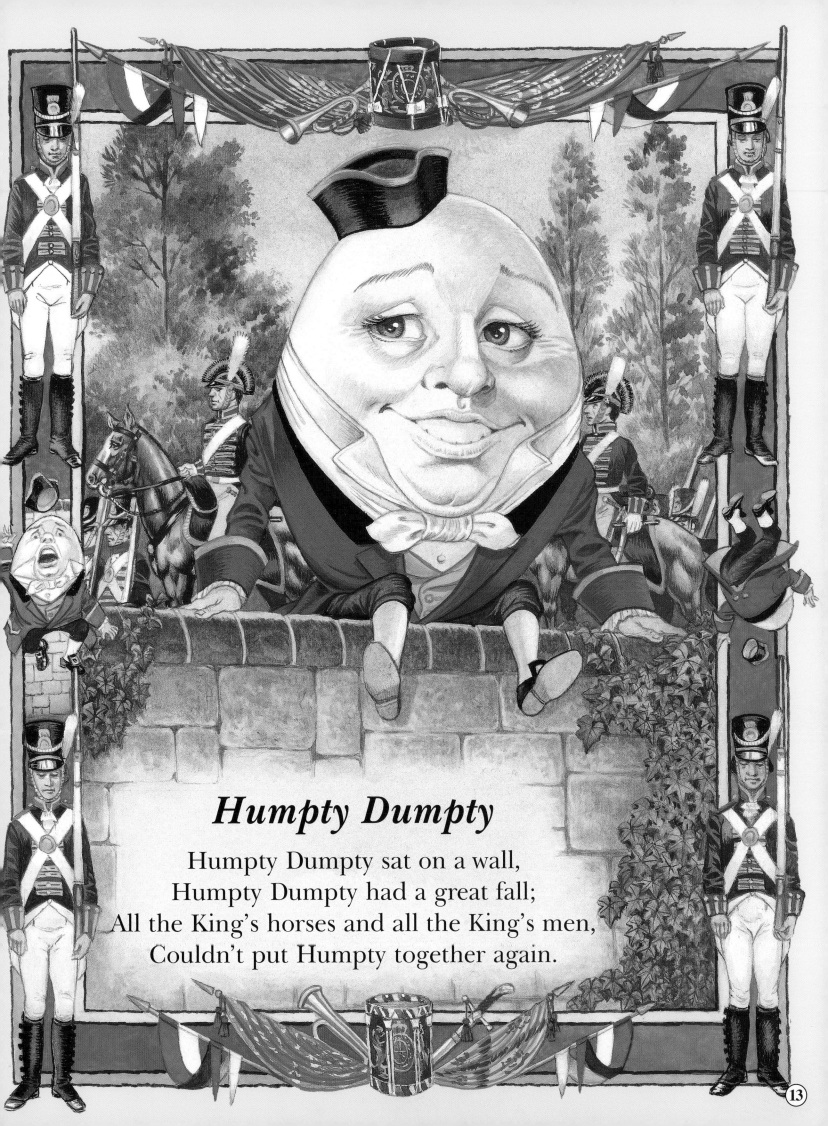

Humpty Dumpty

Humpty Dumpty sat on a wall,
Humpty Dumpty had a great fall;
All the King's horses and all the King's men,
Couldn't put Humpty together again.

I Had a Little Nut Tree

I had a little nut tree,
Nothing would it bear
But a silver nutmeg
And a golden pear

The King of Spain's daughter
Came to visit me,
And for all the sake
Of my little nut tree.

Mary, Mary

Mary, Mary, quite contrary,
How does your garden grow?
With silver bells,
And cockle shells,
And pretty maids all in a row.

Rock-a-Bye Baby

Rock-a-bye baby,
On a tree-top,
When the wind blows
The cradle will rock.

When the bow breaks,
The cradle will fall -
Down will come baby,
Cradle and all.

See-Saw Margery Daw

See-saw Margery Daw,
Johnny shall have a new master;
He shall have but a penny a day,
Because he can't work any faster.

The Grand Old Duke of York

Oh, the grand old Duke of York,
He had ten thousand men;
He marched them up
To the top of the hill,
And he marched them down again.

And when they were up they were up,
And when they were down they were down,
And when they were only half way up,
They were neither up nor down.

Jack and Jill

Jack and Jill
Went up the hill,
To fetch a pail of water;
Jack fell down,
And broke his crown,
And Jill came tumbling after.

Then up Jack got,
And home did trot,
As fast as he could caper.
He went to bed,
To mend his head
With vinegar and brown paper.

Tom the Piper's Son

Tom, Tom, the piper's son,
Stole a pig and away did run;
The pig was eat,
And Tom was beat,
And Tom went howling down the street.

Diddle, Diddle, Dumpling

Diddle, diddle, dumpling, my son John,
Went to bed with his trousers on;
One shoe off and one shoe on,
Diddle, diddle, dumpling, my son John.

Little Boy Blue

Little Boy Blue,
Come blow your horn,
The sheep's in the meadow,
The cow's in the corn.

Where is the boy
Who looks after the sheep?
He's under the haystack,
Fast asleep.

Little Jack Horner

Little Jack Horner sat in the corner,
Eating a Christmas pie;
He put in his thumb,
And pulled out a plum,
And said: "What a good boy am I?"

Polly Flinders

Little Polly Flinders
Sat among the cinders,
Warming her pretty little toes;
Her mother came and caught her,
And smacked her little daughter,
For spoiling her nice new clothes.

Old King Cole

Old King Cole
Was a merry old soul,
And a merry old soul was he;
He called for his pipe,
And he called for his bowl,
And he called for his fiddlers three.

Every fiddler had a fine fiddle,
And a very fine fiddle had he;
Oh, there's none so rare
As can compare
With King Cole and his fiddlers three.

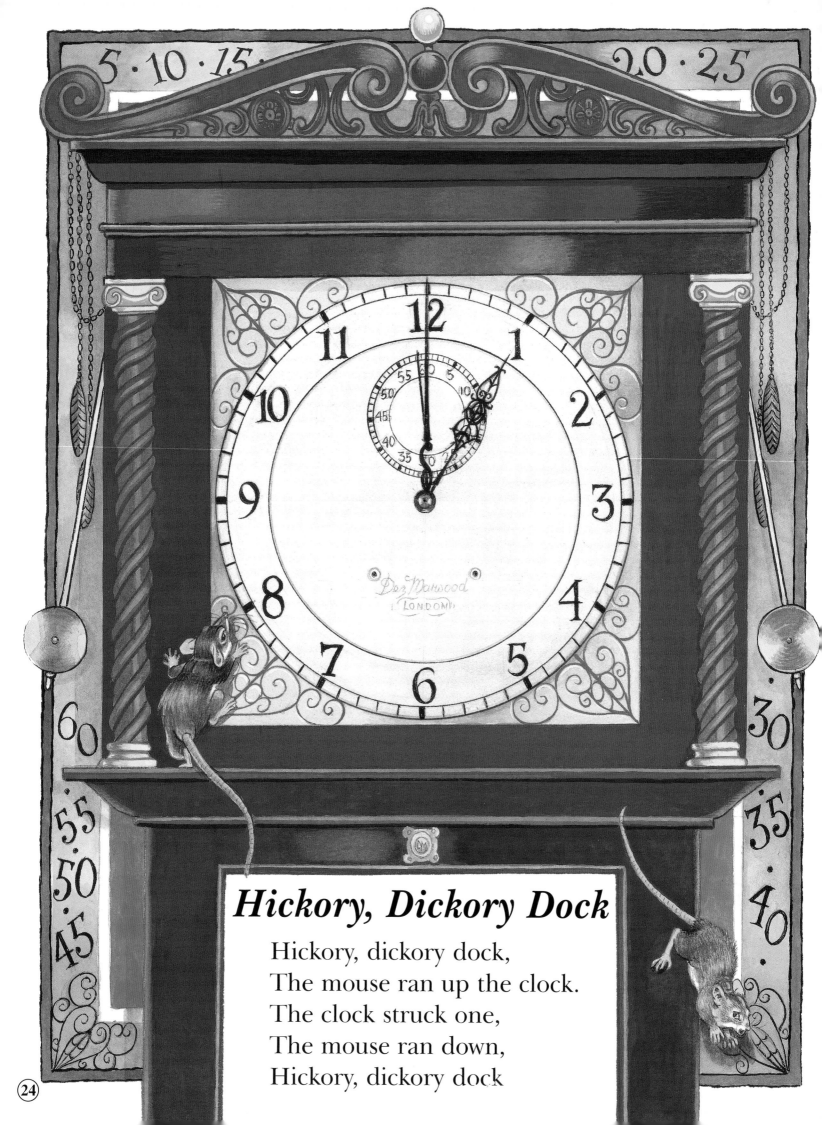

Hickory, Dickory Dock

Hickory, dickory dock,
The mouse ran up the clock.
The clock struck one,
The mouse ran down,
Hickory, dickory dock

Old Mother Hubbard

Old Mother Hubbard
Went to the cupboard,
To get her poor dog a bone;
But when she got there,
The cupboard was bare,
And so the poor dog had none.

Polly Put the Kettle On

Polly put the kettle on,
Polly put the kettle on,
Polly put the kettle on,
We'll all have tea.

Sukey take it off again,
Sukey take it off again,
Sukey take it off again,
They've all gone away.

Goosey Gander

Goosey, goosey gander,
Where shall I wander?
Upstairs and downstairs,
In my lady's chamber.
Where I met an old man,
Who wouldn't say his prayers,
I took him by the left leg,
And threw him down the stairs.

Here We Go Round the Mulberry Bush

Here we go round the mulberry bush,
The mulberry bush, the mulberry bush,
Here we go round the mulberry bush,
On a cold and frosty morning.

This is the way we wash our hands,
Wash our hands, wash our hands,
This is the way we wash our hands,
On a cold and frosty morning.

This is the way we clean our teeth,
This is the way we clean our teeth,

Clean our teeth, clean our teeth,
On a cold and frosty morning.

This is the way we brush our hair,
Brush our hair, brush our hair,
This is the way we brush our hair,
On a cold and frosty morning.

This is the way we go to school,
Go to school, go to school,
This is the way we go to school,
On a cold and frosty morning.

Sing a Song of Sixpence

Sing a song of sixpence,
A pocket full of rye;
Four and twenty blackbirds
Baked in a pie.

When the pie was opened,
The birds began to sing;
Wasn't that a dainty dish
To set before the King

The King was in his
counting-house,
Counting out his money,
The Queen was in the parlour,
Eating bread and honey.

The maid was in the garden,
Hanging out the clothes,
When down came a blackbird
And pecked off her nose.

Little Miss Muffet

Little Miss Muffet
Sat on a tuffet,
Eating her curds and whey;
There came a big spider,
Who sat down beside her,
And frightened
Miss Muffet away.